l

Pr

and

Blessings

Bishops' Committee on the Liturgy
National Conference of Catholic Bishops
United States Catholic Conference
Washington, D.C.

In its planning document, as approved by the general membership of the National Conference of Catholic Bishops in November 1987, the Bishops' Committee on the Liturgy was authorized to prepare a book of prayers and blessings for use by Catholic families and households. *Daily Prayers and Blessings* is excerpted from that book *Catholic Household Blessings and Prayers*, which was approved by the NCCB Administrative Committee in March 1988, and is authorized for publication by the undersigned.

Reverend Robert N. Lynch
General Secretary
July 10, 1989   NCCB/USCC

Contents

FOREWORD

The heart of renewal is prayer. And the key to renewing prayer is enkindling a love and practice of prayer in the hearts of those who make up the Church. Roman Catholics, like any people who share a faith and a way of life, need the words and gestures that express that faith and teach that way of life.

This book of prayers is offered so that all Catholics may have access to their heritage and may come to know the prayers that are both their duty and their privilege. It is meant to be a way of reminding and a way of learning what belongs to us. For all who make up the Church, these prayers and rites are something that we take with reverence for all the generations that have shaped them for us. We will give something of ourselves to these prayers, something that they yet lack, something that can form Christians in our time and place. Then we will hand them on, for they are not finally ours. They belong to the communion of saints in which we walk and in which our children walk and their children may also walk.

Finally, whether we say, "God bless you," or join in a rite of song and prayer and Scripture, we are proclaiming the good news of God's love and reign.

THE CHURCH'S PRAYER

The Lord's Prayer, either sung or recited by one person alone or by many assembled, is the foundation of the Church's daily prayer. In these words from Matthew, chapter 6, the baptized people bless the Lord's name and pray for God's kingdom, for daily bread, and for forgiveness. Even when no other prayers can be prayed, this one is commended to each Christian to be used in the morning, during the day, and at night. The first translation is that commonly used by Roman Catholics. The second is a translation now shared by Catholics and many other English-speaking Christians. The third text is the shorter version of the Lord's Prayer found in the gospel of Luke (11:2-4).

Our Father, who art in heaven,
hallowed be thy name;
thy kingdom come;
thy will be done on earth as it is in
heaven.
Give us this day our daily bread;
and forgive us our trespasses
as we forgive those who trespass
against us;
and lead us not into temptation,
but deliver us from evil.
Amen.

Our Father in heaven,
   hallowed be your name,
   your kingdom come,
   your will be done,
   on earth as in heaven.
Give us today our daily bread.
Forgive us our sins
   as we forgive those who sin against us.
Save us from the time of trial
   and deliver us from evil.
For the kingdom, the power, and the glory are
   yours,
   now and for ever.
Amen.

Father, hallowed be your name,
   your kingdom come.
   Give us each day our daily bread
   and forgive us our sins,
   for we ourselves forgive everyone in debt to
   us,
   and do not subject us to the final test.

WAKING

Upon waking, make the sign of the cross and say:

In the name of the Father, and of the Son, and of the Holy Spirit. Amen.

Or trace a small cross on the lips and say:

Lord, open my lips,
and my mouth will proclaim your praise.

FOR EVERY DAY

Glory to the Father, and to the Son, and to the
  Holy Spirit:
as it was in the beginning, is now, and will be for
  ever.
(Amen.)

Gloria Patri

Holy, holy, holy Lord, God of power and might,
heaven and earth are full of your glory.
Hosanna in the highest.

Sanctus

Hear, O Israel!
The Lord is our God, the Lord alone!
Blessed is God's glorious kingdom for ever and
  ever.
You shall love the Lord, your God, with all your
  mind,
and with all your soul, and with all your
  strength.

Sh'ma Israel

FOR SUNDAY

Glory to God in the highest,
   and peace to his people on earth.

Lord God, heavenly King,
almighty God and Father,
   we worship you, we give you thanks,
   we praise you for your glory.

Lord Jesus Christ, only Son of the Father,
Lord God, Lamb of God,
you take away the sin of the world:
   have mercy on us;
you are seated at the right hand of the Father:
   receive our prayer.
For you alone are the Holy One,
you alone are the Lord,
you alone are the Most High,
   Jesus Christ,
   with the Holy Spirit,
   in the glory of God the Father. Amen.

Gloria in excelsis Deo

WHEN OPENING THE EYES

Blessed are you, Lord, God of all creation:
you open the eyes of the blind.

WHEN RISING

Blessed are you, Lord, God of all creation:
you raise up those who are bowed down.

Blessed are you, Lord, God of all creation:
you set captives free.

Awake, O sleeper,
and arise from the dead,
and Christ will give you light.

Ephesians 5:14

I arise today
through God's strength to pilot me,
God's might to uphold me,
God's wisdom to guide me,
God's eye to look before me,
God's ear to hear me,
God's hand to guard me,
God's way to lie before me,
God's shield to protect me,
God's hosts to save me from the snares of the
    devil.

Saint Patrick's Breastplate

WASHING AND DRESSING

Blessed are you, Lord, God of all
     creation:
you take the sleep from my eyes
and the slumber from my eyelids.

Blessed are you, Lord, God of all
     creation:
you clothe the naked.

Bless, O Christ, my face.
Let my face bless everything.
Bless, O Christ, my eyes.
Let my eyes bless all they see.

Blessed are you, Lord, God of all
     creation:
you formed us in wisdom
and gave us the paths and
     openings in our bodies.

FOR LENT

Have mercy on me, O God, in your goodness;
　　in the greatness of your compassion wipe out
　　my offense.
Thoroughly wash me from my guilt
　　and of my sin cleanse me.

Let me hear the sounds of joy and gladness;
　　the bones you have crushed shall rejoice.
Turn away your face from my sins,
　　and blot out all my guilt.

A clean heart create for me, O God,
　　and a steadfast spirit renew within me.
Cast me not out from your presence,
　　and your holy spirit take not from me.

Psalm 51:3-4,10-13 (*Miserere*)

FOR EASTERTIME AND SUNDAYS

Give thanks to the LORD, for he is good,
　　for his mercy endures forever.

I was hard pressed and was falling,
   but the LORD helped me.
My strength and my courage is the LORD,
   and he has been my savior.

You are my God, and I give thanks to you;
   O my God, I extol you.
Give thanks to the LORD, for he is good;
   for his kindness endures forever.

Psalm 118:1,13-14,28-29

FOR ALL OTHER DAYS

*The Benedictus (Canticle of Zechariah) is an
ancient morning prayer. It is customary to make
the sign of the cross during the first words.*

+ Blessed be the Lord, the God of Israel;
he has come to his people and set them free.

He has raised up for us a mighty savior,
born of the house of his servant David.

Through his holy prophets he promised of old,
   that he would save us from our enemies,
   from the hands of all who hate us.

He promised to show mercy to our fathers
and to remember his holy covenant.

This was the oath he swore to our father
   Abraham:

to set us free from the hands of our enemies,
free to worship him without fear
holy and righteous in his sight all the days of our
life.

You, my child, shall be called the prophet of the
Most High
for you will go before the Lord to prepare his
way,

to give his people knowledge of salvation
by the forgiveness of their sins.

In the tender compassion of our God
the dawn from on high shall break upon us,
to shine on those who dwell in darkness
and the shadow of death,
and to guide our feet into the way of peace.

Luke 1:68-79 (*Benedictus*)

GOING OUT FROM HOME EACH DAY

Blessed are you, Lord, God of all
   creation:
you guide my footsteps.

Blessed are you, Lord, God of all
   creation:
you spread out the earth upon the
   waters.

Direct our steps to yourself, O God,
and show us how to walk in charity and peace.

Praise the LORD from the heavens,
    praise him in the heights;
Praise him, all you his angels,
    praise him, all you his hosts.
Praise him, sun and moon;
    praise him, all you shining stars.
Praise him, you highest heavens,
    and you waters above the heavens.
Let them praise the name of the LORD,
    for he commanded and they were created;
He established them forever and ever;
    he gave them a duty which shall not pass
    away.

Praise the LORD from the earth,
    you sea monsters and all depths;
Fire and hail, snow and mist,
    storm winds that fulfill his word;
You mountains and all you hills,
    you fruit trees and all you cedars;
You wild beasts and all tame animals,
    you creeping things and you winged fowl.

Let the kings of earth and all peoples,
  the princes and all the judges of the earth,
Young men too, and maidens,
  old men and boys,
Praise the name of the LORD,
  for his name alone is exalted;
His majesty is above earth and heaven,
  and he has lifted up the horn of his people.
Be this his praise from all his faithful ones,
  from the children of Israel, the people
    close to him.   Alleluia.

Psalm 148

Come, let us sing joyfully to the LORD;
  let us acclaim the Rock of our salvation.
Let us greet him with thanksgiving;
  let us joyfully sing psalms to him.
For the LORD is a great God,
  and a great king above all gods;
In his hands are the depths of the earth,
  and the tops of the mountains are his.
His is the sea, for he has made it,
  and the dry land, which his hands have
    formed.

Come, let us bow down in worship;
  let us kneel before the LORD who made us.
For he is our God,
  and we are the people he shepherds,
    the flock he guides.

Psalm 95:1-7

FOR THE DAY'S WORK AT HOME

God be in my head, and in my understanding;
God be in my eyes, and in my looking;
God be in my mouth, and in my speaking;
God be in my heart, and in my thinking;
God be at my end, and at my departing.

AT NOON

V. The angel spoke God's message to Mary,
R. and she conceived of the Holy Spirit.
Hail, Mary. . . .

V. "I am the lowly servant of the Lord:
R. let it be done to me according to your word."
Hail, Mary. . . .

V. And the Word became flesh
R. and lived among us.
Hail, Mary. . . .

V. Pray for us, holy Mother of God,
R. that we may become worthy of the promises of Christ.

Let us pray.

Lord,
fill our hearts with your grace:
once, through the message of an angel
you revealed to us the incarnation of your
    Son;
now, through his suffering and death
lead us to the glory of his resurrection.

We ask this through Christ our Lord.
R. Amen.

The Angelus

*This is also prayed in the early morning and at
evening.*

*The Hail Mary is an ancient prayer whose first
verses come from Luke's gospel, the words of the
angel and the words of Elizabeth. The final lines
invoke Mary's protection in the present moment
and at the time of death.*

TAKING FOOD AND DRINK

BEFORE EATING AND DRINKING

Bless + us, O Lord, and these
  your gifts
which we are about to receive from
  your goodness.
Through Christ our Lord.
R. Amen.

AFTER EATING AND DRINKING

We give you thanks for all your
  gifts, almighty God,
living and reigning now and for
  ever.
R. Amen.

Hail Mary, full of grace,
the Lord is with you!
Blessed are you among women,
and blessed is the fruit of your womb, Jesus.
Holy Mary, Mother of God,
pray for us sinners,
now and at the hour of our death.
Amen.

Blessed are you, Lord, God of all creation:
you bring forth bread from the earth.

God is blessed in all his gifts
and holy in all his works,
who lives and reigns for ever and ever.
R. Amen.

All the world hopes in you, O Lord,
that you will give us food in our hunger.
You open wide your hand
and we are filled with good things.

Cf. Psalm 104

Blessed be the Lord,
of whose bounty we have received
and by whose goodness we live.

The poor shall eat and shall have their fill.
Those who long for the Lord shall give him
   praise.
May their hearts live for ever.

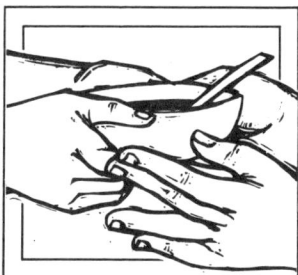

LABOR, SERVICE, STUDY, AND ALMSGIVING

May God be glorified in all things
through Jesus Christ.

Cf. 1 Peter 4:11

May the peace of God that is
    beyond all understanding
guard our hearts and our thoughts
    in Christ Jesus.

Cf. Philippians 4:7

We give you thanks, our Father!
You call us to share the lot of the
saints in light!

Cf. Colossians 1:12

IN DEEDS OF SERVICE

In all our words and actions
let us give thanks to God
in the name of the Lord Jesus.

Cf. Colossians 3:17

May God put our faith into action,
to work in love, to persevere in hope,
through our Lord Jesus Christ.

Cf. 1 Thessalonians 1:3

WHEN GIVING OR RECEIVING ALMS

May God fully supply all our needs
according to his generosity, with magnificence,
in Christ Jesus!
To God be glory for ever and ever!

Cf. Philippians 4:19-20

Blessed are you, Lord, God of tenderness and
   compassion,
rich in kindness and faithfulness.

Cf. Exodus 34:6

God of the humble and help of the oppressed:
Blessed are you, Lord!
Support of the weak and refuge of the forsaken:
Blessed are you, Lord!

Cf. Judith 9:11

AT WORK

Day by day we bless you, Lord.
We praise your name for ever.

Jesus, gentle and humble of heart, have mercy
   on us.
Mary, mirror of justice, pray for us.
Joseph, model of workers, pray for us.

May we know the shortness of our days,
that we may learn wisdom.

Lord,
may everything we do
begin with your inspiration
and continue with your help
so that all our prayers and works
may begin in you
and by you be happily ended.

We ask this through Christ our Lord.
R. Amen.

AT STUDY

Teach me to do your will, for you are my God.

Psalm 143:10

[May] we grow in grace and in the knowledge
of our Lord and savior Jesus Christ.
To him be glory now and to the day of eternity

2 Peter 3:18

COMING HOME
EACH DAY

Hear us, Lord,
and send your angel from heaven
to visit and protect,
to comfort and defend
all who live in this house.

May the Lord of peace give us
peace
all the time and in every way.
The Lord be with us.

Cf. 2 Thessalonians 3:16

O radiant Light, O Sun divine,
Of God the Father's deathless face,
O Image of the light sublime
That fills the heav'nly dwelling
place.

Lord Jesus Christ, as daylight
fades,

As shine the lights of eventide,
We praise the Father with the Son,
The Spirit blest and with them one.

O Son of God, the source of life,
Praise is your due by night and day;
Our [untarnished] lips must raise the
  strain
Of your proclaimed and splendid name.

Ancient Greek Hymn for Evening: "*Phos Hilaron*"

FOR EVENING DURING LENT

Truly you have formed my inmost being;
  you knit me in my mother's womb.
I give you thanks that I am fearfully, wonderfully
  made;
  wonderful are your works.

Probe me, O God, and know my heart;
  try me, and know my thoughts;
See if my way is crooked,
  and lead me in the way of old.

Psalm 139:13-14,23-24

FOR EVENING ON SUNDAY AND DURING EASTERTIME

Alleluia! Praise the Lord, all you nations;
glorify him, all you peoples!
For steadfast in his kindness toward us,
and the fidelity of the Lord endures forever.

Psalm 117

ON ALL OTHER DAYS

> *The Magnificat (Canticle of Mary) is an ancient*
> *evening prayer. It is customary to make the sign*
> *of the cross during the first words.*

+ My soul proclaims the greatness of the Lord,
my spirit rejoices in God my Savior;
for he has looked with favor on his lowly
   servant.

From this day all generations will call me blessed:
the Almighty has done great things for me,
and holy is his Name.

He has mercy on those who fear him
in every generation.

He has shown the strength of his arm,
he has scattered the proud in their conceit.

He has cast down the mighty from their thrones,
and has lifted up the lowly.

He has filled the hungry with good things,
and the rich he has sent away empty.

He has come to the help of his servant Israel
for he has remembered his promise of mercy,
the promise he made to our fathers,
to Abraham and his children for ever.

Luke 1:46-55 (*Magnificat*)

AT TABLE

When all are seated, begin with the sign of the cross:

In the name of the Father, and of the Son, and of the Holy Spirit. Amen.

If several pray together, they may alternate the verses:

[The eyes of all creatures] look to
  you to give them food in
    due time.
When you give it to them, they
  gather it;
  when you open your hand,
  they are filled with good things.

Psalm 104:27-28

The leader says:

Let us call on the name of the Father,
who always takes care of his children.

All pray together:

Our Father. . . .

For the kingdom, the power, and the
    glory are yours,
now and for ever.

Bless + us, O Lord, and these your gifts
which we are about to receive from your
    goodness.
Through Christ our Lord.
R. Amen.

*One of the following prayers may be used instead
of "The eyes of all creatures look to you":*

Lord, the lover of life,
you feed the birds of the skies
and array the lilies of the field.
We bless you for all your creatures
and for the food we are about to receive.
We humbly pray that in your goodness
you will provide for our brothers and sisters
who are hungry.

We ask this through Christ our Lord.
R. Amen.

Blessed are you, almighty Father,
who give us our daily bread.
Blessed is your only begotten Son,
who continually feeds us on the word of life.
Blessed is the Holy Spirit,
who brings us together at this table of love.
Blessed be God now and for ever.
R. Amen.

Bread may be lifted up and broken:

Blessed are you, Lord, God of all creation:
you bring forth bread from the earth.
Blessed be God for ever.

All respond:

Blessed be God for ever.

A cup of wine may be lifted up:

Blessed are you, Lord, God all creation:
creator of the fruit of the vine.
Blessed be God for ever.

All respond:

Blessed be God for ever.

This blessing may be sung to any appropriate tune such as "The Old Hundreth" (Praise God from Whom All Blessings Flow):

Be present at our table, Lord.
Be here and everywhere adored.
Thy creatures bless and grant that we
may feast in Paradise with thee.

One of the following prayers may be used instead of "Bless us, O Lord":

Lord, our God,
with fatherly love you come to the aid of your
    children.
Bless us and these your gifts
which we are about to receive from your
    goodness.
Grant that all peoples may be gladdened
by the favors of your providence.

We ask this through Christ our Lord.
R. Amen.

God of all goodness,
through the breaking of bread together
you strengthen the bonds that unite us in love.
Bless + us and these your gifts.
Grant that as we sit down together at table
in joy and sincerity,
we may grow always closer in the bonds of love.

We ask this through Christ our Lord.
R. Amen.

May your gifts refresh us, O Lord,
and your grace give us strength.
R. Amen.

THANKSGIVING AFTER MEALS

Let all your works praise you,
  O Lord.
Let all your people bless you.

All pray together:

We give you thanks for all your
  gifts, almighty God,
living and reigning now and for
  ever.
R. Amen.

For the sake of your name,
  O Lord,
reward those who have been good
  to us
and give them eternal life.
R. Amen.

Or:

Lord, give all people the food they need,
so that they may join us in giving you
thanks.
R. Amen.

*When members of the household are absent, the
leader concludes:*

May God be with us
and with N. (and N.)
R. Amen.

One or more of these prayers may be used instead:

The leader says:

Blessed be the name of the Lord.

All respond:

Now and forever.

We thank you, O Lord, the giver of all good
    gifts,
who have kindly brought us together at this
    table.
Refreshed in body, may we make our earthly
    journey in joy
and one day arrive at the banquet table of
    heaven.

We ask this through Christ our Lord.
R. Amen.

We thank you, our God,
for the food you have given us.
Make our sharing this bread together
lead to a renewal of our communion with you,
with one another, and with all creatures.

We ask this through Christ our Lord.
R. Amen.

Lord, you feed every living thing.
We have eaten together at this table; keep us in
    your love.
Give us true concern for the least of our sisters
    and brothers,
so that as we gladly share our food with them,
we may also sit down together with them
at the table of the kingdom of heaven.

We ask this through Christ our Lord.
R. Amen.

Lord, you have fed us from your gifts and favors;
fill us with your mercy,
for you live and reign for ever and ever.
R. Amen.

God is blessed in all his gifts
and holy in all his works,
who lives and reigns for ever and ever.
R. Amen.

AT TABLE
ON SUNDAY

One person lights a candle and says:

Jesus Christ is the light of the
world.

All respond:

A light no darkness can
overpower.

The leader lifts up the bread and prays:

We thank you, Father,
for the life and knowledge you
    have revealed to us
through your child Jesus.
Glory be yours through all ages.
As grain once scattered on the
    hillside
was in this broken bread made
    one,
so from all lands may we be
    gathered
into your kingdom by your Son.

The Didache

All respond "Amen" to each blessing; parents may place their hands on their children as they bless them:

The Lord bless us and keep us.
R. Amen.
The Lord's face shine upon us and be
   gracious to us.
R. Amen.
The Lord look upon us with kindness and
   give us peace.
R. Amen.

Then an acclamation or song may be sung.

Praise God from whom all blessings flow.
Praise God all creatures here below.
Praise God above, ye heavenly host.
Praise Father, Son and Holy Ghost.

AT TABLE ON DAYS OF FASTING AND ALMSGIVING

O LORD, hear my prayer,
and let my cry come to you.
Hide not your face from me
in the day of my distress.
Incline your ear to me;
in the day when I call, answer
me speedily.
For my days vanish like smoke,
and my bones burn like fire.
Withered and dried up like grass is
my heart;
I forget to eat my bread.

I am sleepless, and I moan;
I am like a sparrow alone on the
housetop.

For I eat ashes like bread
and mingle my drink with tears.

My days are like a lengthening shadow,
   and I wither like grass.
But you, O LORD, abide forever,
   and your name through all generations.

Psalm 102:2-5,8,10,12-13

ON FRIDAYS

All praise be yours, God our Creator,
as we wait in joyful hope
for the flowering of justice
and the fullness of peace.
All praise for this day, this Friday.
By our weekly fasting and prayer,
cast out the spirit of war, of fear and mistrust,
and make us grow hungry for human kindness,
thirsty for solidarity with all the people of your
   dear earth.
May all our prayer, our fasting, and our deeds
be done in the name of Jesus.
R. Amen.

AT TABLE DURING ADVENT

*Advent candles may be lighted
as the leader says:*

Blessed are you, Lord, God
  of all creation:
in the darkness and in the light.

Blessed are you
in this food and in our sharing.

Blessed are you as we wait
  in joyful hope
for the coming of our savior,
  Jesus Christ.

All respond:

For the kingdom, the power, and the
glory are yours, now and for ever.

The leader says:

Come, Lord Jesus!

All respond:

Come quickly!

Another form of Advent prayer begins with the sign of the cross.

In the name of the Father, and of the Son, and of the Holy Spirit. Amen.

Someone at table reads one of the following Scriptures or the Scripture assigned to the liturgy of the day.

A Listen to the words of the prophet Isaiah:

Trust in the LORD forever!
   For the LORD is an eternal Rock.
He humbles those in high places,
   and the lofty city he brings down;
He tumbles it to the ground,
   levels it with the dust.
It is trampled underfoot by the needy,
   by the footsteps of the poor.

Isaiah 26:4-6

Or:

B Listen to the words of the prophet
Isaiah:

I am the LORD and there is no other,
there is no God besides me.

I form the light, and create the
darkness,
I make well-being and create woe;
I, the Lord, do all these things.
Let justice descend, O heavens, like dew
from above,
like gentle rain let the skies drop it
down.
Let the earth open and salvation bud
forth;
let justice also spring up!
I, the LORD, have created this.

Isaiah 45:5a,7-8

The reader concludes:

This is the Word of the Lord.

All respond:

Thanks be to God.

46

The leader invites:

Lift up your hearts.

All respond:

We lift them up to the Lord.

Then the leader prays:

God, the Father of mercies,
you willed your Son to take flesh,
in order to give life back to us.
Bless these your gifts
with which we are about to nourish our
    bodies,
so that, receiving new strength, we may
    wait in watchfulness
for the glorious coming of Christ.

We ask this through the same Christ our
    Lord.
R. Amen.

AFTER THE MEAL

The leader says:

Let us live soberly, justly, and devoutly in
    this world
as we wait in joyful hope
for the coming of our Savior, Jesus Christ.

All respond:

For the kingdom, the power, and the
glory are yours, now and for ever.

On the last days before Christmas, the following
prayers are added:

December 17:
O Wisdom, O holy Word of God,
you govern all creation with
    your strong yet tender care.
Come and show your people the way to
    salvation.

December 18:
O sacred Lord of ancient Israel,
who showed yourself to Moses in the burning
    bush,
who gave him the holy law on Sinai mountain:
come, stretch out your mighty hand to set us
    free.

December 19:
O Flower of Jesse's stem,
you have been raised up as a sign for all peoples;
kings stand silent in your presence;
the nations bow down in worship before you.
Come, let nothing keep you from coming to our
    aid.

December 20:
O Key of David, O royal Power of Israel
    controlling at your will the gate of heaven:
come, break down the prison walls of death
    for those who dwell in darkness and the
        shadow of death;
and lead your captive people into freedom.

December 21:
O Radiant Dawn, splendor of eternal light,
　　sun of justice:
come, shine on those who dwell in darkness
　　and the shadow of death.

December 22:
O King of all the nations,
the only joy of every human heart;
O Keystone of the mighty arch of humankind,
come and save the creature you fashioned from
　　the dust.

December 23:
O Emmanuel, king and lawgiver,
desire of the nations,
Savior of all people,
come and set us free, Lord our God.

AT TABLE DURING CHRISTMASTIME

A Christmas candle may be lighted as the leader says:

Glory to God in the highest.

All respond:

And peace to his people on earth.

The leader prays:

Lord Jesus,
in the peace of this season
our spirits rejoice:
With the beasts and angels,
the shepherds and stars,
with Mary and Joseph
we sing God's praise.

By your coming
may the hungry be filled with
    good things,
and may our table and home be
    blessed.

Glory to God in the highest.

All respond:

And peace to his people on earth.

Another form of Christmas prayer begins with the sign of the cross.

In the name of the Father, and of the Son, and of the Holy Spirit. Amen.

Someone at table reads one of the following Scriptures or the text assigned to the liturgy of the day.

A Listen to the words of the holy gospel according to John:

And the Word became flesh
and made his dwelling among us,
and we saw his glory,

the glory as of the Father's only Son,
full of grace and truth.

John 1:14

Or:

B Listen to the words of the prophet
Isaiah:

I rejoice heartily in the LORD,
   in my God is the joy of my soul;
For he has clothed me with a robe of
   salvation,
   and wrapped me in a mantle of justice,
Like a bridegroom adorned with a
   diadem,
   like a bride bedecked with her jewels.
As the earth brings forth its plants,
   and a garden makes its growth spring
   up,
So will the LORD GOD make justice and
   praise
   spring up before all the nations.

Isaiah 61:10-11

The reader concludes:

This is the Word of the Lord.

Thanks be to God.

The leader invites:

Lift up your hearts.

All respond:

We lift them up to the Lord.

Then the leader prays:

Blessed are you, Lord God.
Through the fruitful virginity of Mary
you fulfilled the long expectation
   of the poor and oppressed.
Grant that with the same faith
   with which Mary awaited the birth of
      her Son,
we may look for him in our brothers and
   sisters in need.

We ask this through Christ our Lord.
R. Amen.

AFTER THE MEAL

The leader says:

The Word became flesh, alleluia.

All respond:

And dwelt among us, alleluia.

AT TABLE DURING THE WEEKDAYS OF LENT

Begin after a short silence. The leader alternates with the others who are present.

V. I was hungry.
R. And you gave me food.

V. I was thirsty.
R. And you gave me drink.

V. I was a stranger.
R. And you welcomed me.

V. I was naked.
R. And you clothed me.

V. I was ill.
R. And you comforted me.

V. I was in jail.
R. And you came to see me.

The leader prays:

Lord Jesus Christ,
may our lenten fasting turn us
    toward all our brothers and sisters who
    are in need.
Bless this table, our good food, and
    ourselves.
Send us through Lent with good cheer,
and bring us to the fullness of your
    passover.
R. Amen.

> *Another form of lenten prayer begins with the
> sign of the cross.*

In the name of the Father, and of the Son,
and of the Holy Spirit. Amen.

> *Someone at table reads one of the following
> Scriptures or the text assigned to the liturgy of
> the day.*

A Listen to the words of the apostle Paul
to the Romans:

I urge you therefore, brothers [and
sisters], by the mercies of God, to offer
your bodies as a living sacrifice, holy and
pleasing to God, your spiritual worship.
Do not conform yourself to this age but be
transformed by the renewal of your mind,
that you may discern what is the will of
God, what is good and pleasing and
perfect.

Romans 12:1-2

Or:

B Listen to the words of the prophet
Isaiah:

Wash yourselves clean!
Put away your misdeeds from before my
eyes;
cease doing evil; learn to do good.
Make justice your aim: redress the
wronged,
hear the orphan's plea, defend the
widow.

Isaiah 1:16-17

Or:

C Listen to the words of the apostle Paul
   to the Corinthians:

[God says:]

"In an acceptable time I heard you,
and on the day of salvation I helped
you."

Behold, now is a very acceptable time;
behold, now is the day of salvation. . . .
In everything we commend ourselves as
ministers of God, through much
endurance, in afflictions, hardships,
constraints, beatings, imprisonments,
riots, labors, vigils, fasts. . . . We are
treated as deceivers and yet are truthful;
as unrecognized and yet acknowledged; as
dying and behold we live; as chastised
and yet not put to death; as sorrowful yet
always rejoicing; as poor yet enriching
many; as having nothing and yet
possessing all things.

2 Corinthians 6:2,4-5,8-10

The reader concludes:

This is the Word of the Lord.

All respond:

Thanks be to God.

The leader invites:

Lift up your hearts.

All respond:

We lift them up to the Lord.

Then the leader prays:

We thank you, O Lord,
who give us this food to eat.
We pray that you may also provide food
for those who are hungry
and gather us all together
at the table of your heavenly kingdom.

We ask this through Christ our Lord.
R. Amen.

AFTER THE MEAL

The leader says:

No one lives on bread alone.

All respond:

But on every word that comes from the mouth of God.

AT TABLE DURING THE EASTER TRIDUUM

From Holy Thursday evening until the great Vigil in the night between Holy Saturday and Easter, the catechumens and the baptized fast and pray and await the celebration of baptism. Any meals are very simple. "Let the paschal fast be kept sacred. Let it be observed everywhere on Good Friday and, where possible, prolonged throughout Holy Saturday, as a way of coming to the joys of the Sunday of the resurrection with uplifted and welcoming heart" (*Constitution on the Sacred Liturgy*, 110). The same prayer is used before and after meals.

For our sake Christ was obedient, accepting even death, death on a cross.

Therefore God raised him on high and gave him the name above all other names.

61

AT TABLE DURING EASTERTIME

An Easter candle is lighted while the leader says:

This is the day the Lord has made, alleluia!

All respond:

Let us rejoice and be glad, alleluia!

The leader prays:

We praise you, Lord, with greater
    joy than ever in this Easter
      season.
The thirsty have come to the
    water.
The poor have come to receive
    bread and eat.
Blessed are you in earth's bounty:
the joy of the resurrection renews
    the whole world.

Christ is risen, alleluia!

All respond:

Christ is truly risen, alleluia!

Another form of Easter prayer begins with the sign of the cross.

In the name of the Father, and of the Son, and of the Holy Spirit. Amen.

Someone at table reads one of the following Scriptures or the text assigned to the liturgy of the day.

A Listen to the words of the holy gospel according to John:

[When the disciples had returned to shore at the Sea of Tiberias,] they saw a charcoal fire with fish on it and bread. Jesus said to them, "Bring some of the fish you just caught." So Simon Peter went over and dragged the net ashore full of one hundred fifty-three large fish. Even though there were so many, the net was not torn. Jesus said to them, "Come, have breakfast." And none of the disciples dared to ask him, "Who are you?" because they realized it was the Lord. Jesus came over and took the bread and gave it to them, and in like manner the fish.

John 21:9-13

Or:

B Listen to the words of the holy gospel according to Luke:

[The two disciples urged Jesus,] "Stay with us, for it is nearly evening and the day is almost over." So he went in to stay with them. And it happened that, while he was with them at table, he took bread, said the blessing, broke it, and gave it to them. With that their eyes were opened and they recognized him.

Luke 24:29-31

Or:

C Listen to the words of the apostle Peter:

Blessed be the God and Father of our
Lord Jesus Christ, who in his great mercy
gave us a new birth to a living hope
through the resurrection of Jesus Christ
from the dead.

1 Peter 1:3

The reader concludes:

This is the Word of the Lord.

All respond:

Thanks be to God.

The leader invites:

Lift up your hearts.

All respond:

We lift them up to the Lord.

We joyfully sing your praises, Lord
    Jesus Christ.
Whom on the day of your resurrection
were recognized by your disciples
    in the breaking of the bread.

Remain here with us
as we gratefully partake of these gifts,
and at the banquet table in heaven
    welcome us,
who have welcomed you in our brothers
    and sisters,
for you live and reign for ever and ever.
Amen.

All join in singing an alleluia.

AFTER THE MEAL

The leader says:

The disciples recognized the Lord,
alleluia.

All respond:

In the breaking of the bread, alleluia.

From Ascension to Pentacost, the leader says:

Lord, send out your Spirit.

All respond:

And renew the face of the earth.

AT BEDSIDE

If several pray together, one leads the first prayers and all pray the Hail Mary together. Begin with the sign of the cross and say:

May the all-powerful Lord grant us a restful night
and a peaceful death.

Protect us, Lord, as we stay awake;
watch over us as we sleep,
that awake, we may keep watch with Christ,
and asleep, rest in his peace.

Hail Mary, full of grace,
the Lord is with you!
Blessed are you among women,
and blessed is the fruit of your womb,
   Jesus.
Holy Mary, Mother of God,
pray for us sinners,
now and at the hour of our death.
R. Amen.

> *A longer form of night prayer begins with silence. This is an examination of conscience, a time to reflect on the day now past. Scripture texts which suggest the content of this examination of conscience include: Exodus 20:1-17; Matthew 5:1-11; Matthew 25:31-46; Ephesians 4:17-32; and Colossians 3:1-17. Then all pray the Confiteor:*

I confess to almighty God,
and to you, my brothers and sisters,
that I have sinned through my own fault
in my thoughts and in my words,
in what I have done,
and in what I have failed to do;

and I ask blessed Mary, ever virgin,
all the angels and saints,
and you, my brothers and sisters,
to pray for me to the Lord our God.

> *Psalm 91, may be prayed. The following
> hymn is also appropriate. It may be sung
> to the tune called "Tallis Canon" or to "The
> Old Hundreth" (Praise God from Whom All
> Blessings Flow), or to another appropriate tune.*

All praise to thee, my God, this night,
For all the blessings of the light;
Keep me, O keep me, King of kings,
Beneath thine own almighty wings.

Forgive me, Lord, for thy dear Son,
The sin that I this day have done,
That with the world, myself and thee,
I, before sleep, at peace may be.

Teach me to live that I may dread
The grave as little as my bed;
Teach me to die that so I may
Rise glorious on that final day.

Thomas Ken

> *The Canticle of Simeon may also be part of night
> prayer:*

Lord, now you let your servant go in peace;
your word has been fulfilled:

my own eyes have seen the salvation
which you have prepared in the sight of every
  people:

a light to reveal you to the nations
and the glory of your people Israel.

Luke 2:29-32 (Nunc Dimittis)

*A period of silence may be observed, and prayers
of intercession and thanksgiving may be offered.*

The leader then prays:

Visit this house,
we beg you, Lord,
and banish from it
the deadly power of the evil one.
May your holy angels dwell here
to keep us in peace,
and may your blessing be always upon us.

We ask this through Christ our Lord.
R. Amen.

Or:

Lord Jesus Christ,
you have given your followers
an example of gentleness and humility,
a task that is easy, a burden that is light.
Accept the prayers and work of this day,
and give us the rest that will strengthen us
to render more faithful service to you
who live and reign for ever and ever.

All invoke the protection of the Blessed Mother:

A Hail, holy Queen, mother of mercy,
hail, our life, our sweetness, and our hope.
To you we cry, the children of Eve;
to you we send up our sighs,
mourning and weeping in this land of exile.
Turn, then, most gracious advocate,
your eyes of mercy toward us;
lead us home at last
and show us the blessed fruit of your womb,
  Jesus:
O clement, O loving, O sweet Virgin Mary.

Salve, Regina

Or:

B Mary, mother whom we bless,
full of grace and tenderness,
defend me from the devil's power
and greet me in my dying hour.

*The day ends, as it began, with the sign of the
cross. A parent may sign a child's forehead or
heart with the cross, saying one of these blessings:*

God bless you.

Praised be Jesus Christ!

The grace of the Lord Jesus be with [us] all.

Revelation 22:21

In the silent hours of night, bless the Lord.

Lord, bless this household and each one.
Place the cross of Christ on us with the power of
   your love
until we see the land of joy.

Christ is shepherd over you,
enfolding you on every side.
Christ will not forsake you hand or foot,
nor let evil come near you.

Other night prayers of parent and child:

Now I lay me down to sleep,
I pray the Lord my soul to keep.
Four corners to my bed,
Four angels there aspread:
Two to foot and two to head,
And four to carry me when I'm dead.
If any danger come to me,
Sweet Jesus Christ deliver me.
And if I die before I wake,
I pray the Lord my soul to take.

Angel sent by God to guide me,
be my light and walk beside me;
be my guardian and protect me;
on the paths of life direct me.

MORNING PRAYER

The following is an example of Morning Prayer for
Sunday as found in the Roman rite for the Liturgy
of the Hours.

V. God, come to my assistance.
R. Lord, make haste to help me.

Glory to the Father, and to the Son,
    and to the Holy Spirit:
as it was the beginning, is now,
    and will be for ever.
Amen. Alleluia.

HYMN

(On Sundays)

On this day, the first of days,
God the Father's name we praise;
Who, creation's Lord and spring,
Did the world from darkness bring.

On this day the eternal Son
Over death his triumph won;
On this day the Spirit came
With his gifts of living flame.

God, the blessed Three in One,
May thy holy will be done;
In thy word our souls are free.
And we rest this day with thee.

On other days, "I Sing as I Arise Today," page 288, or another appropriate hymn may be sung.

Psalmody

Antiphon 1   As morning breaks I look to you,
O God, to be my strength this day,
alleluia.

Psalm 63:2-9

O God, you are my God, for you I long;
for you my soul is thristing.
My body pines for you
like a dry, weary land without water.
So I gaze on you in the sanctuary
to see your strength and your glory.

For your love is better than life,
my lips will speak your praise.
So I will bless you all my life,
in your name I will lift up my hands.
My soul shall be filled as with a banquet,
my mouth shall praise you with joy.

On my bed I remember you.
On you I muse through the night
for you have been my help;
in the shadow of your wings I rejoice.
My soul clings to you;
your right hand holds me fast.

Glory to the Father, and to the Son,
and to the Holy Spirit:
as it was the beginning, is now,
and will be for ever.
Amen.

Psalm-prayer

Father, creator of unfailing light, give that same light to those who call to you. May our lips praise you; our lives proclaim your goodness; our work give you honor, and our voices celebrate you for ever.

Antiphon 1   As morning breaks I look to you, O God, to be my strength this day, alleluia.

Antiphon 2   From the midst of the flames the three young men cried out with one voice: Blessed be God, alleluia.

Daniel 3:57-88, 56

Bless the Lord, all you works of the Lord.
Praise and exalt him above all forever.
Angels of the Lord, bless the Lord.
You heavens, bless the Lord.
All you waters above the heavens, bless the Lord.
All you hosts of the Lord, bless the Lord.
Sun and moon, bless the Lord.
Stars of heaven, bless the Lord.

Every shower and dew, bless the Lord.
All you winds, bless the Lord.
Fire and heat, bless the Lord.
Cold and chill, bless the Lord.
Dew and rain, bless the Lord.
Frost and chill, bless the Lord.
Ice and snow, bless the Lord
Nights and days, bless the Lord.

Light and darkness, bless the Lord.
Lightnings and clouds, bless the Lord.

Let the earth bless the Lord.
Praise and exalt him above all forever.
Mountains and hills, bless the Lord.
Everything growing from the earth, bless the
    Lord.
You springs, bless the Lord.
Seas and rivers, bless the Lord.
You dolphins and all water creatures, bless the
    Lord.
All you birds of the air, bless the Lord.
All you beasts wild and tame, bless the Lord.
You sons of men, bless the Lord.

O Israel, bless the Lord.
Praise and exalt him above all forever.
Priests of the Lord, bless the Lord.
Servants of the Lord, bless the Lord.
Spirits and souls of the just, bless the Lord.
Holy men of humble heart, bless the Lord
Hananiah, Azariah, Mishael, bless the Lord.
Praise and exalt him above all forever.

Let us bless the Father, and the Son, and the
    Holy Spirit.
Let us praise and exalt him above all forever.
Blessed are you, Lord, in the firmament of
    heaven.
Praiseworthy and glorious and exalted above all
    forever.

Antiphon 2   From the midst of the flames the
three young men cried out with one
voice: Blessed be God, alleluia.

Antiphon 3   Let the people of Zion rejoice in their
King, alleluia.

Psalm 149

Sing a new song to the Lord,
his praise in the assembly of the faithful.
Let Israel rejoice in its maker,
let Zion's sons exult in their king.
Let them praise his name with dancing
and make music with timbrel and harp.

For the Lord takes delight in his people.
He crowns the poor with salvation.
Let the faithful rejoice in their glory,
shout for joy and take their rest.
Let the praise of God be on their lips
and a two-edged sword in their hand,

to deal out vengeance to the nations
and punishment on all the peoples;
to bind their kings in chains
and their nobles in fetters of iron;
to carry out the sentence pre-ordained;
this honor is for all his faithful.

Glory to the Father, and to the Son,
and to the Holy Spirit:
as it was the beginning, is now,
and will be for ever.
Amen.

Psalm-prayer

Let Israel rejoice in you, Lord, and acknowledge
you as creator and redeemer. We put our trust in
your faithfulness and proclaim the wonderful
truths of salvation. May your loving kindness
embrace us now and for ever.

Antiphon 3   Let the people of Zion rejoice in their
                King, alleluia.

Reading   Revelation 7:10,12

Salvation comes from our God, who is seated on
the throne, and from the Lamb! Amen. Blessing
and glory, wisdom and thanksgiving, honor,
power, and might be to our God forever and
ever. Amen.

Silence

Response to the Word of God

V. Christ, Son of the living God, have mercy on
   us.
R. Christ, Son of the living God, have mercy on
   us.

V. You are seated at the right hand of the Father,
R. have mercy on us.

V. Glory to the Father, and to the Son, and to the Holy Spirit.

R. Christ, Son of the living God, have mercy on us.

Canticle of Zechariah   Luke 1:68-79

+ Blessed be the Lord, the God of Israel;
he has come to his people and set them free.

He has raised up for us a mighty savior,
born of the house of his servant David.

Through his holy prophets he promised of old
    that he would save us from our enemies,
    from the hands of all who hate us.

He promised to show mercy to our fathers
and to remember his holy covenant.

This was the oath he swore to our father
    Abraham:
to set us free from the hands of our enemies,
free to worship him without fear,
holy and righteous in his sight all the days of our
    life.

You, my child, shall be called the prophet of the
    Most High;
for you will go before the Lord to prepare his
    way,
to give his people knowledge of salvation
by the forgiveness of their sins.

In the tender compassion of our God
the dawn from on high shall break upon us,
to shine on those who dwell in darkness and the
    shadow of death,
and to guide our feet into the way of peace.

Glory to the Father, and to the Son,
    and to the Holy Spirit:
as it was in the beginning, is now,
    and will be for ever.
Amen.

Intercessions

Christ is the sun that never sets, the true light
that shines on every person. Let us call out to
him in praise:

R. Lord, you are our life and our salvation.

Creator of the stars, we thank you for your gift,
the first rays of the dawn, and we commemorate
your resurrection. R.

May your Holy Spirit teach us to do your will
today, and may your Wisdom guide us always. R.

Each Sunday give us the joy of gathering as your
people, around the table of your word and your
body. R.

From our hearts we thank you, for your countless blessings. R.

Our Father. . . .

Concluding Prayer (The opening prayer from the Sunday Mass or the following prayer is then said.)

Father of love,
hear our prayers.
Help us to know your will
and to do it with courage and faith.

Grant this through our Lord Jesus Christ,
    your Son,
who lives and reigns with you and the
    Holy Spirit,
one God, for ever and ever.
R. Amen.

Dismissal

May the Lord bless us,
protect us from all evil
and bring us to everlasting life.
R. Amen.

EVENING PRAYER

The following is an example of Evening Prayer (Vespers) for Sunday as found in the Roman rite for the Liturgy of the Hours.

V. God, come to my assistance.
R. Lord, make haste to help me.

Glory to the Father, and to the Son,
    and to the Holy Spirit:
As it was in the beginning, is now,
    and will be for ever.
Amen. Alleluia.

Hymn (for example: "O Radiant Light,"
        page 46).

Psalmody

Antiphon 1   Like burning incense, Lord, let my
              prayer rise up to you.

Psalm 141

I have called to you, Lord; hasten to help me!
Hear my voice when I cry to you.
Let my prayer arise before you like incense,
the raising of my hands like an evening oblation.

Set, O Lord, a guard over my mouth;
keep watch, O Lord, at the door of my lips!
Do not turn my heart to things that are wrong,
to evil deeds with those who are sinners.

Never allow me to share in their feasting.
If the upright strike or reprove me it is kindness;
but let the oil of the wicked not anoint my head.
Let my prayer be ever against their malice.

Their leaders were thrown down by the side of
    the rock;
then they understood that my words were kind.
As a millstone is shattered to pieces on the
    ground,
so their bones were strewn at the mouth of the
    grave.

To you, Lord God, my eyes are turned;
in you I take refuge; spare my soul!
From the trap they have laid for me keep me
    safe;
keep me from the snares of those who do evil.

Let the wicked fall into the traps they have set
whilst I pursue my way unharmed.

Psalm-prayer

Lord, from the rising of the sun to its setting
your name is worthy of all praise. Let our prayer
come like incense before you. May the lifting up
of our hands be as an evening sacrifice acceptable
to you, Lord our God.

Antiphon 1 Like burning incense, Lord, let my
prayer rise up to you.

Antiphon 2 You are my refuge, Lord; you are all
that I desire in life.

Psalm 142

With all my voice I cry to the Lord,
with all my voice I entreat the Lord.
I pour out my trouble before you;
I tell you all my distress
while my spirit faints within me.
But you, O Lord, know my path.

On the way where I shall walk
they have hidden a snare to entrap me.
Look on my right and see:
there is not one who takes my part.
I have no means of escape,
not one who cares for my soul.

I cry to you, O Lord.
I have said: "You are my refuge,
all I have left in the land of the living."
Listen then to my cry
for I am in the depths of distress.

Rescue me from those who pursue me
for they are stronger than I.
Bring my soul out of this prison
and then I shall praise your name.
Around me the just will assemble
because of your goodness to me.

Glory to the Father, and to the Son,
  and to the Holy Spirit:
as it was the beginning, is now,
  and will be for ever.
Amen.

Psalm-prayer

Lord, we humbly ask for your goodness. May
you help us to hope in you, and give us a share
with your chosen ones in the land of the living.

Antiphon 2   You are my refuge, Lord; you are all
                that I desire in life.

Antiphon 3   The Lord Jesus humbled himself,
                and God exalted him for ever.

Canticle   Philippians 2:6-11

+ Though he was in the form of God,
Jesus did not deem equality with God
something to be grasped at.

Rather, he emptied himself
and took the form of a slave,
being born in the likeness of men.

He was known to be of human estate,
and it was thus that he humbled himself,
obediently accepting even death,
death on a cross!

Because of this,
God highly exalted him
and bestowed on him the name
above every other name,

so that at Jesus' name
every knee must bend
in the heavens, on the earth,
and under the earth,
and every tongue proclaim
to the glory of God the Father:
JESUS CHRIST IS LORD!

Reading   Romans 11:33-36

Oh, the depth of the riches and wisdom and
knowledge of God! How inscrutable are his
judgments and how unsearchable his ways!
  "For who has known the mind of the Lord
    or who has been his counselor?"
  "Or who has given him anything
    that he may be repaid?"
For from him and through him and for him are
all things. To him be glory forever. Amen.

Silence

Response to the Word of God

V. Our hearts are filled with wonder
   as we contemplate your works, O Lord.
R. Our hearts are filled with wonder
   as we contemplate your works, O Lord.

V. We praise the wisdom which wrought them
   all,
R. as we contemplate your works, O Lord.

V. Glory to the Father, and to the Son,
   and to the Holy Spirit:
R. Our hearts are filled with wonder
   as we contemplate your works, O Lord.

Canticle of Mary   Luke 1:46-55

+ My soul proclaims the greatness of the Lord,
my spirit rejoices in God my Savior
for he has looked with favor on his lowly
   servant.

From this day all generations will call me blessed:
the Almighty has done great things for me,
and holy is his Name.

He has mercy on those who fear him
in every generation.

He has shown the strength of his arm,
he has scattered the proud in their conceit.

He has cast down the mighty from their thrones,
and has lifted up the lowly.

He has filled the hungry with good things,
and the rich he has sent away empty.

He has come to the help of his servant Israel
for he has remembered his promise of mercy,
the promise he made to our fathers,
to Abraham and his children for ever.

Glory to the Father,
   and to the Son, and to the Holy Spirit:
as it was in the beginning, is now,
   and will be for ever.
Amen.

Intercessions

We give glory to the one God—Father, Son, and
Holy Spirit—and in our weakness we pray:

R. Lord, be with your people.

Holy Lord, Father all-powerful, let justice spring
up on the earth then your people will dwell in
the beauty of peace. R.

Let every nation come into your kingdom, so that
all peoples will be saved. R.

Let married couples live in your peace, and grow
in mutual love. R.

Reward all who have done good to us, Lord, and
grant them eternal life. R.

Look with compassion on victims of hatred and
war, grant them heavenly peace. R.

Our Father. . . .

Concluding Prayer (The opening prayer from the Sunday Mass or the following prayer is then said.)

Lord,
guide the course of world events
and give your Church the joy and peace
of serving you in freedom.

We ask this through our Lord Jesus Christ,
    your Son,
who lives and reigns with you and the
    Holy Spirit,
one God, for ever and ever.
R. Amen.

Dismissal

May the Lord bless us,
protect us from all evil
and bring us to everlasting life.
R. Amen.

ACKNOWLEGMENTS

"All praise be yours, God our Creator . . ." *Prayers for Fridays,* copyright © 1983, the Archdiocese of Chicago, Liturgy Training Publications. Used by permission.

"As grain once scattered on the hillside . . ." Excerpt from "Father, We Thank Thee" by F. Bland Tucker in *The Hymnal 1982,* copyright © Church Pension Fund, The Church Hymnal Corporation. Used by permission.

"God be in my head and in my understanding . . ." Excerpt from *The Oxford Book of Prayer,* copyright © 1985 Oxford University Press. Used by permission.

"O radiant Light, O Sun divine . . ." *Phos Hilaron* in *Morning Praise and Evensong,* translation and copyright © by William G. Storey. Used by permission.

"Blessed are you, Lord, God of all creation . . ." and "Christ is shepherd over you . . ." Excerpts from *Carmina Gadelica,* Vol. I, by Alexander Carmichael. Copyright © Scottish Academic Press Limited. Used by permission.